My Journal of

God's Healing in GRIEF

by
Ron and Kathleen Duncan

My Journal of God's Healing in Grief
by Ron and Kathleen Duncan

© 2016 Ron and Kathleen Duncan
Published by Precept Ministries International
P.O. Box 182218
Chattanooga, TN 37421
www.precept.org
ISBN 978-1-62119-712-6

2016—Second Edition
Printed in the United States of America

CONTENTS

My Journal of God's Healing in Grief

If you have experienced the death of a loved one, you know the pain and anguish of grief. You know that the loss of some you care for deeply can shake your faith to its core.

We understand the horrendous heartache of losing not only our parents and many friends but also of losing a son. In the wee hours of the morning of August 13, 2013, we heard the knock at the door, and received the chilling news from police officer Wiggins that our 20-year-old son Andrew had been killed in a car wreck.

The shocking news brought about shattered dreams, and sad, sobering times for our family. Over the past three years, we have walked through our sadness and into healing, hope, peace and joy. We believe it was only God and the study of His Word that brought us healing. We want to share that healing and hope with you.

In **God's Healing in Grief** we wrote about our grief journey and how studying God's Word helped us. This 18-lesson study contains Bible study activities to help you learn Truth straight from the Bible. It's designed for you to come to a place of healing by studying for yourself what Scripture says about these important topics. The lessons will gently bring you to a place, not of false comfort found in trite platitudes, but to the solid foundation of Christ and the true comfort found only in God and His Word.

Throughout the study you will find *Just Journaling* prompts designed to help you dig deeper into what you are thinking, feeling, and learning as you study what the Bible says about *God's Healing in Grief*.

This Companion Journal is designed to be used alongside that study; it contains the *Just Journaling* prompts from the book and much more.

Here's a list of prompts we'll use in this *Journal:*

 "Before You Begin" activities to help you think through where you are in grief and what you already know about the topic of the lesson.

 Write what you learned and what you want to remember from the study. This icon often indicates a *Just Journaling* prompt from **God's Healing in Grief.**

 Space to make lists as directed by the *Just Journaling* prompts.

 Space for you to write your thoughts, questions, and feelings about what you learn in the **God's Healing in Grief** study.

 Prompts to write prayers and honestly express what is in your heart to God.

 Pages for lists and summaries of what you learned from studying God's Word. Space for you to copy any scripture passages that touched you in a special way.

In the back of this Journal you will find pages for your lists of *"What I Learned About God"* and *"Who I Am In Christ."* These lists will be a precious resource for you in the years to come.

As you work thorugh the study, it is helpful to look at where you are in your grief journey, to "check in" and see what God has done in you. Periodically, you will be asked how you are doing or what changes you have seen since you started this study. Your answer can be as long or short as you need it to be.

As you write in this Journal be honest. It is *your* **Journal of God's Healing in Grief.** It is just between you and God. Be sure to date Journal entries so you can go back later and see how God worked in your life.

As you work through the study **God's Healing in Grief** write out what you learn and what you're thinking and feeling in this Journal. You may want to express your thoughts in prayers, poetry, and/or drawings. You may want to compose a song that expresses your pain but also your victories amid your grief journey.

You will have victories in grief, but grief itself is not something to be conquered, but rather it is something that is normal and natural, something we go through and feel when we lose someone we love.

From our experience, a Journal to write or draw in is extremely helpful for processing grief and accompanying emotions, thoughts, and questions. This Journal is designed to help do this as you walk through your grief journey.

We pray that you find healing and hope in Christ Jesus as you work through the study and as you write in this Journal.

Precious in the sight of the Lord is the death of his saints (Psalm 116:15).

Who and What I Am Grieving

 Write about the person you lost. Share memories, pictures, newspaper clippings. Write about your love for them. You may want to write out some of the things you miss about them. Your loved one may no longer be here physically, but they matter . . . to you and to God. Your love for them remains with you.

Blessed are those who mourn, for they shall be comforted (Matthew 5:4).

Who and What I Am Grieving

He heals the brokenhearted and binds up their wounds (Psalm 147:3).

Where Am I Today?

 Before you begin studying **God's Healing in Grief,** write about:

- Thoughts and feelings you have about grief and healing

- Questions you have about death and heaven

- What you hope to learn from this study

Comfort in Grief

 Are you willing to let God work in you and lead you? If you are, begin by writing a prayer. Ask the Holy Spirit to teach you, comfort you, and lead you into a place of healing and peace.

Come to me, all who labor and are heavy laden, and I will give you rest (Matthew 11:28).

Write what healing might look like to you. If you can't imagine healing and joy right now, that's okay. Be honest about your thoughts and feelings.

Blessed is the man who remains steadfast under trial, for when he has stood the test he will receive the crown of life, which God has promised to those who love him (James 1:12).

Summarize what you learned about God's Comfort.

May the God of hope fill you with all joy and peace in believing, so that by the power of the Holy Spirit you may abound in hope (Romans 15:13).

You've just looked at verses about God's love and comfort. How are you feeling about what you learned? Write your feelings and thoughts about God and His comfort in light of your loss. What impact do you think this understanding will make in your life?

He heals the brokenhearted and binds up their wounds (Psalm 147:3).

Lesson 1 Wrap Up

 Write out:

1. What you want to remember about God's comfort from Lesson 1

2. What you want to apply in your life

3. What touched your heart

Verses to Remember

Why Study the Bible When I'm Grieving?

 Take time to answer these questions:

Do you regularly study the Bible?

Since your loss have you found it difficult to read the Bible or pray?

Where do you believe your help comes from?

Do you believe God can bring healing to broken hurting people?

What benefits do you see in studying the Bible?

All Scripture is breathed out by God and profitable for teaching, for reproof, for correction, and for training in righteousness, that the man of God may be complete, equipped for every good work (2 Timothy 3:16-17).

Beloved, always begin your study of this book with prayer. Today, write a prayer asking God to show you His truth as you go through this study. Ask Him to reveal Himself to you.

Now may the Lord of peace himself give you peace at all times in every way.
The Lord be with you all (2 Thessalonians 3:16).

At the end of Lesson Two, we suggested a prayer based on truths found in Psalm 119. After reading the passages from this Psalm write your own prayer; or, write a poem about the Word and why we should study the Bible during grief.

Let your steadfast love comfort me according to your promise to your servant. Let your mercy come to me, that I may live; for your law is my delight (Psalm 119:76-77).

Lesson 2 Wrap Up

• Write out what you want to remember from Lesson 2

• What do you want to apply in your life?

• What touched your heart?

Write out any verses that touched you in a special way.

Do You Still Believe?

 Take time to answer two questions in the form of a prayer, poem, or drawing.

- Do you trust God even though you do not understand everything He is doing or why things happen?

- Do you know His love?

. . . but God shows his love for us in that while we were still sinners, Christ died for us (Romans 5:8).

Who Owns & Rules Over All?

 Summarize what you learned about God's Sovereignty over the days of our lives.

Who owns and rules over all?

Remember, this *Journal* is the place where you can be completely honest. Considering your loved one's death, how are you feeling about God ruling overall and numbering our days?

What do you think about all your days being written in God's book? Is this a comfort to you, or does it give you angst?

Your eyes saw my unformed substance; in your book were written, every one of them, the days that were formed for me, when as yet there was none of them (Psalm 139:16).

What questions do you still have about God's nature? Are you willing to have the Holy Spirit show you from Scripture? You may want to write out a prayer. Ask God to reveal Himself to you.

O Lᴏʀᴅ, make me know my end and what is the measure of my days;
let me know how fleeting I am! (Psalm 39:4).

How are you feeling about what you learned?

What impact do you think this understanding will make in your life?

How are you doing this week? Do you feel stuck in your grief?

 Write out your thoughts, questions, and feelings. Pour out your heart to God. He loves you.

Know therefore that the Lord your God is God, the faithful God who keeps covenant and steadfast love with those who love him and keep his commandments, to a thousand generations (Deuteronomy 7:9).

Lesson 3 Wrap Up

- Write out what you want to remember from Lesson 3.

- What do you want to apply in your life?

- What touched your heart?

- Add to your list of *"What I Learned About God."*

Write out any verses from Lesson 3 that touched you in a special way.

Is It Okay to Be Sad?

 Answer these questions in the form of a prayer, poem, or drawing.

- What have you been taught about grief?

- Do you believe that if you are strong you will not be sad?

- Is grief a sign of weakness?

- What expectations have you placed on yourself regarding your grief?

- Do you think these expectations are realistic?

Blessed are those who mourn, for they shall be comforted (Matthew 5:4).

How Some People in the Bible Grieved

 Summarize what you learned about how some in the Bible grieved. Note anything that relates to how you grieve.

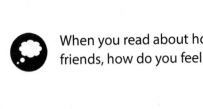 When you read about how Jesus responded to the deaths of His friends, how do you feel? Write what helps you when you are sad.

Do you sometimes want to be alone in your grief? Do you want to just get away from everyone around you? Do you think Jesus understands this?

Based on scriptures we looked at in Lesson 4 do you believe God understands that you are sometimes so sad about the death of your loved one that you want to isolate yourself?

For we do not have a high priest who is unable to sympathize with our weaknesses, but one who in every respect has been tempted as we are, yet without sin (Hebrews 4:15).

Read Job 1-3. Do you have some of the same thoughts and feelings Job expressed?

 Write how you feel. Draw a picture or write a poem.

And they sat with him on the ground seven days and seven nights, and no one spoke a word to him, for they saw that his suffering was very great (Job 2:13).

In the Psalms you studied in this lesson, the psalmist always comes back to trusting and praising God. Look up additional psalms of David. What does he know about God that you want to know and understand?

For his anger is but for a moment, and his favor is for a lifetime. Weeping may tarry for the night, but joy comes with the morning (Psalm 30:5).

How have you responded to sorrow, fear, and grief? Is this how you want to respond? If not, talk to God and ask Him to change the way you're responding to suffering.

Trust in the Lord with all your heart, and do not lean on your own understanding.In all your ways acknowledge him, and he will make straight your paths (Proverbs 3:5-6).

Sadness, Grief, & Mourning

 Summarize what you learned about sadness, grief, and mourning.

If you are hurting today, if you are grieving today, pray; express your sorrow and pain; pour out your heart to Our Heavenly Father who loves you with an everlasting love. He cares for you. He wants to heal your broken heart and help you find joy and peace. His peace is available to all who seek Him.

Surely he has borne our griefs and carried our sorrows; yet we esteemed him stricken, smitten by God, and afflicted. But he was pierced for our transgressions; he was crushed for our iniquities; upon him was the chastisement that brought us peace, and with his wounds we are healed (Isaiah 53:4-5).

Lesson 4 Wrap Up

- Write out what you want to remember about grief and God from Lesson 4.

- What do you want to apply in your life?

- What touched your heart?

- Add to your list *"What I Learned About God."*

Write out any verses from Lesson 4 that touched you in a special way.

We Grieve Differently . . . Together

 Write a prayer. Ask God to give you ears to hear and eyes to see what He wants to teach you in this lesson.

Out of the depths I cry to you, O Lord! O Lord, hear my voice! Let your ears be attentive to the voice of my pleas for mercy! (Psalm 130:1-2)

Do those around you grieve the same way you do? Has there been any conflict surrounding the way you each grieve? How have you handled your different ways of grieving?

Have you found it difficult to treat others with compassion and kindness during your grief? Write what you learned about your behavior as you studied this lesson. If you need to confess anything to God, do so. Write about it and ask God for forgiveness.

We who are strong have an obligation to bear with the failings of the weak, and not to please ourselves. Let each of us please his neighbor for his good, to build him up.

May the God of endurance and encouragement grant you to live in such harmony with one another, in accord with Christ Jesus, that together you may with one voice glorify the God and Father of our Lord Jesus Christ. Therefore welcome one another as Christ has welcomed you, for the glory of God (Romans 15:1-2, 5-7).

Is someone you care about in sin? As they grieve, are they lashing out or doing harm to themselves? Could you pray for them? Consider making a list of ways you can help and gently restore them.

Brothers, if anyone is caught in any transgression, you who are spiritual should restore him in a spirit of gentleness. Keep watch on yourself, lest you too be tempted (Galatians 6:1).

Have you judged others in the way they grieved? Have you tried to get others to grieve as you do rather than allowing them to grieve in ways that help them? If so, write about it. Confess your wrongs to God. Ask Him to forgive you. He promises that if we confess our sins, He is faithful and just to forgive us and cleanse us from all unrighteousness.

Rejoice with those who rejoice, weep with those who weep. Live in harmony with one another. Do not be haughty, but associate with the lowly. Never be wise in your own sight (Romans 12:15-16).

How can others help you in your grief? Make a list of specific things you would like others to do for you. This will be a great tool for when someone says "If there is anything I can do to help . . . ." You will have a ready answer.

 Make a second list of ways you can help those around you who are also grieving. Try to do one thing for someone who is grieving this week. It may be as simple as a hug, a smile, or a prayer. Maybe you can write them a note of encouragement or get them a small gift to help them feel loved. Bear one another's burdens!

I have been crucified with Christ. It is no longer I who live, but Christ who lives in me. And the life I now live in the flesh I live by faith in the Son of God, who loved me and gave himself for me (Galatians 2:20).

Judging How Others Grieve

 Summarize what you learned about judging others.

Judge not, that you be not judged (Matthew 7:1).

Compassion vs. Comparing

 Summarize what you learned about compassion and comparing.

Lesson 5 Wrap Up

• Write out what you want to remember from Lesson 5.

• What do you want to apply in your life?

• What touched your heart?

• Add to your list *"What I Learned About God."*

Write out any verses from Lesson 5 that touched you in a special way.

Why Do People Die?

In Lesson 6 you will study some difficult passages. Take time to ask God to help understand His Word. Write out your prayer. Tell God how you are doing and what you are thinking and feeling today.

The earth is the Lord's and the fullness thereof, the world and those who dwell therein, for he has founded it upon the seas and established it upon the rivers (Psalm 24:1-2).

"Did my loved one die because God needed another angel?" . . . and other wrong sayings.

 Has anyone said some of the platitudes listed in this lesson to you? Did you believe them before this study? Summarize what you learned about each of the following questions.

Did this happen because of my sin? Am I being punished for some sin?

Did my loved one die because God needed another angel?

Do people die so that someone can eventually "get saved!"?

Do those we love die because God causes evil?

Often, we who are grieving get angry with others when they say stupid or hurtful things. But bitterness does not help us heal in grief. Do you need to forgive someone? Write about it and do it today!

And Jesus said, "Father, forgive them, for they know not what they do"
(Luke 23:34).

So why do people die?

 Summarize what you learned about why people die.

Eternal Life

 Summarize what you learned about eternal life and what Jesus did for you.

Before you go on with this lesson, take time to think about what you just learned. How are you feeling about what you learned about why people die? What questions about death do you still have?

Whoever believes in the Son has eternal life . . . (John 3:36).

If you are already a believer, write about your faith. How has your faith impacted your grief?

If you want to become a believer today, write about your desire to become a child of God. Confess anything you need to confess and ask God to save you from sin and death. He will.

. . . but God shows his love for us in that while we were still sinners, Christ died for us (Romans 5:8).

Lesson 6 Wrap Up

- Write out what you want to remember about why people die and eternal life from Lesson 6.

- What do you want to apply in your life?

- What touched your heart?

- Add to your list *"What I Learned About God."*

Write out any verses from Lesson 6 that touched you in a special way.

But Why *This* Person *I* Love at *This* Time?

 Look back at your *"What I Learned about God"* list. Who do you believe God is? What do you believe about His nature?

For my thoughts are not your thoughts, neither are your ways my ways, declares the Lord. For as the heavens are higher than the earth, so are my ways higher than your ways and my thoughts than your thoughts (Isaiah 55:8-9).

Beloved, what are you thinking? How do you feel about God number-ing our days? Does this make you uncomfortable or comfortable?

Since his days are determined, and the number of his months is with you, and you have appointed his limits that he cannot pass (Job 14:5).

Based on what you've studied in this lesson, what do you believe about the reasons your loved one died? Do you find comfort in knowing God is sovereign? Write out your thoughts, questions, and feelings. Maybe write a poem or song.

For everything there is a season, and a time for every matter under heaven: a time to be born, and a time to die; (Ecclesiastes 3:1-2).

Why Death Came into the World

 This may seem like a strange journaling assignment but it will help you as you grieve. It's good to review what we learn and write it down. Make a list of everything you learned about why death came into the world and who controls life and death. This will also give you a resource to come back to when you have questions in the future.

Lesson 7 Wrap Up

 • Write out what you want to remember from Lesson 7.

• What do you want to apply in your life?

• What touched your heart?

• Add to your list of *"What I Learned About God. "*

 Write out any verses from Lesson 7 that touched you in a special way.

Could I Have Prevented My Loved One's Death?

 Think about the events surrounding your loved one's death. Do you feel responsible in any way for the death? Do you have regrets about events and your actions during that time?

Remember, your journal is for your eyes only, between you and God. Be honest. Many times we feel guilt or regret even when we were not responsible for what happened.

If any of you lacks wisdom, let him ask God, who gives generously to all without reproach, and it will be given to him. But let him ask in faith, with no doubting, for the one who doubts is like a wave of the sea that is driven and tossed by the wind (James 1:5-6).

Write in your Journal any feelings of guilt or shame regarding any responsibility you have or had for the death of your loved one. Write a prayer asking God to show you the truth regarding any part you may have played in the death.

If you had no responsibility in the death you are grieving, write that here.

 Summarize anything you learned from Scripture that you want to remember about Satan, anything that will help your healing in grief.

And no wonder, for even Satan disguises himself as an angel of light
(2 Corinthians 11:14).

Are you feeling guilt or shame regarding a death for which you hold no responsibility? Did you play a role in a death but not through sin? If so, write about your feelings. Then write the truth about what happened. Talk to God and ask Him to help you remember the truth regarding the situation.

For God so loved the world, that he gave his only Son, that whoever believes in him should not perish but have eternal life (John 3:16).

If you sinned and caused a death, write the truth about forgiveness. You may want to look up additional verses regarding what Jesus did for you and the forgiveness that is available to you. If you need to confess anything to God, do so. Ask forgiveness. Write that "today" you have been forgiven.

Against you, you only, have I sinned and done what is evil in your sight, so that you may be justified in your words and blameless in your judgment (Psalm 51:4).

If the last words you spoke to a loved one who died were in anger or if you feel shame over the way you treated them and you can't shake the guilt, write it down as a confession, an apology, to the person and to God. Pour out your heart, everything that is troubling your conscience. Then read it aloud to God. Tell Him you are sorry and ask His forgiveness.

If we say we have no sin, we deceive ourselves, and the truth is not in us. If we confess our sins, he is faithful and just to forgive us our sins and to cleanse us from all unrighteousness (1 John 1:8-9)

Lesson 8 Wrap Up

 • Write out what you want to remember from Lesson 8.

• What do you want to apply in your life?

• What touched your heart?

• Add to your list *"What I Learned About God. "*

 Write out any verses from Lesson 8 that touched you in a special way.

Welcoming God's Transformation in Grief

 If you have not kept up with your list of *"What I Learned About God,"* now is a good time to update it; then, on this page, write what you're thinking and feeling about God today. How has what you have learned impacted your healing in grief?

For we who live are always being given over to death for Jesus' sake, so that the life of Jesus also may be manifested in our mortal flesh (2 Corinthians 4:11).

These next few assignments may take you some time to complete. Don't rush through this *Just Journaling* assignment! Let the Holy Spirit show you marvelous things!

 First, looking back over you learned in the first part of this study, what has impacted you the most? What surprised or comforted you the most?

And after you have suffered a little while, the God of all grace, who has called you to his eternal glory in Christ, will himself restore, confirm, strengthen, and establish you (1 Peter 5:10).

<u>Second,</u> what changes have you seen in your grief over the weeks you have been studying God's Word? Are you seeing God's healing in your grief? Describe what you are seeing. Maybe draw a picture or write a poem.

Not only that, but we rejoice in our sufferings, knowing that suffering produces endurance, and endurance produces character, and character produces hope, and hope does not put us to shame, because God's love has been poured into our hearts through the Holy Spirit who has been given to us (Romans 5:3-5).

<u>Finally,</u> if you are willing to work out what God is working in as He transforms you, write about it.

Write a prayer asking God to continue to work in and through you.

Do not be conformed to this world, but be transformed by the renewal of your mind, that by testing you may discern what is the will of God, what is good and acceptable and perfect (Romans 12:2).

Lesson 9 Wrap Up

 • Write out what you want to remember from Lesson 9.

• What do you want to apply in your life?

• What touched your heart?

• Add to your list of *"What I Learned About God. "*

 Write out any verses from Lesson 9 that touched you in a special way.

Changing Our Thoughts

 How have your thoughts impacted your conversations and your actions in grief? What do you spend most of your time thinking about? What thoughts keep you awake at night?

For those who live according to the flesh set their minds on the things of the flesh, but those who live according to the Spirit set their minds on the things of the Spirit (Romans 8:5).

Colossians 3

 Summarize what you learned from Colossians 3 by listing all the things to put off and away and put on. Ask God to help you apply what you have learned.

Do Not Fear

 Summarize what you learned about fear from the lesson. Record verses you found in your Bible's concordance or online.

Take time to write a prayer to God, expressing your concerns and fears. Maybe you'd prefer to write a poem or draw a picture that represents your fears and how God can help you conquer them.

Are you afraid of losing another family member or friend? Look up "fear" and "fear not" in your Bible's concordance or in an online one. Copy some of these verses onto this page, then turn them into a prayer or poem, asking God to help you trust Him and not fear.

You keep him in perfect peace whose mind is stayed on you, because he trusts in you. Trust in the LORD forever, for the LORD GOD is an everlasting rock (Isaiah 26:3-4).

Philippians 4:4-9

 Read Philippians 4:4-9. Summarize the key points of this passage.

Below is the list of godly attributes from Philippians 4:8. Under each write something you can choose to think about when dark thoughts creep into your mind. Make a list of good things in your life. Make a list of things other than your pain and grief that you can think about when you begin to feel anxious, angry, fearful, or upset. Add to this list over the next few weeks.

True

Honorable

Just

Pure

Lovely

Commendable

Excellent

Praiseworthy

Finally, brothers, whatever is true, whatever is honorable, whatever is just, whatever is pure, whatever is lovely, whatever is commendable, if there is any excellence, if there is anything worthy of praise, think about these things (Philippians 4:8).

Lesson 10 Wrap Up

- Write out what you want to remember about your thoughts from Lesson 10.

- What do you want to apply in your life?

- What touched your heart?

- Add to your list *"What I Learned About God. "*

Write out any verses from Lesson 10 that touched you in a special way.

Gratitude in Grief

 In the last lesson you looked at changing your thoughts. How are you doing with this? Have you been able to think about good things in your life? Where are you in your healing process today?

Rejoice always, pray without ceasing, give thanks in all circumstances; for this is the will of God in Christ Jesus for you (1 Thessalonians 5:16-18).

Have you found yourself bitter about your loss rather than grateful about what you **had, have,** and ***will have*** in Christ? Do you think you can begin to rejoice in God? Can you rejoice because of what Jesus did for you? Write what you're thinking and feeling after studying these passages.

Give thanks to the Lord, for he is good, for his steadfast love endures forever (Psalm 136:1).

We must work to change our thoughts. We must practice thankfulness for it to become a part of our daily lives. How are you doing in this area? Do you thank God for the gifts He has given you? Do you share with others the wonderful things He has done for you?

Oh give thanks to the Lord, for he is good, for his steadfast love endures forever! Let the redeemed of the Lord say so, whom he has redeemed from trouble (Psalm 107:1-2).

Gratitude List

 List things you're grateful for today. It can be as simple as "Life, My Family, Christ's Love."

Gratitude List

Gratitude List

Three Things I Am Grateful For (Annual)

1. Something I am grateful for *from my loved one's life*

2. Something I am grateful for *in my loved one's death*

3. Something I am grateful for *since my loved one's death*

Lesson 11 Wrap Up

- Write out what you want to remember about gratitude from Lesson 11.

- What do you want to apply in your life?

- What touched your heart?

- Add to your list of *"What I Learned About God."*

Write out any verses from Lesson 11 that touched you in a special way.

How Should We React When Others Hurt Us?

 How are you doing with what you've learned in the first eleven lessons? When you think back to your earliest days in grief, what things stick out in your mind? Do you remember kind things people did for you or hurtful things they said and did? What do you remember most?

For if you forgive others their trespasses, your heavenly Father will also forgive you, but if you do not forgive others their trespasses, neither will your Father forgive your trespasses (Matthew 6:14-15).

Kind Things People Did and Said

Begin a list of kind things people did for you and kind things they said to you during your grief. Add at least five things to this list today.

Pray and thank God for them and for what they did. Add to this list whenever someone does something kind for you.

I therefore, a prisoner for the Lord, urge you to walk in a manner worthy of the calling to which you have been called, with all humility and gentleness, with patience, bearing with one another in love, eager to maintain the unity of the Spirit in the bond of peace (Ephesians 4:1-3).

In the lesson, Kathleen shared about her resentments and need to forgive. Is there someone you need to forgive? Pray and talk to God about it. Forgive him or her and ask the Lord to help you walk that out. Write your thoughts about the situation considering the passages you've studied. Then write the person a letter, extending your forgiveness if he or she sinned against you. You may not need to send it at all, but writing it out will help you.

For if you forgive others their trespasses, your heavenly Father will also forgive you, but if you do not forgive others their trespasses, neither will your Father forgive your trespasses (Matthew 6:14-15).

How to Speak to and Treat Others

 Summarize what you learned about speech and how to treat others.

If your brother sins against you, go and tell him his fault, between you and him alone. If he listens to you, you have gained your brother (Matthew 18:15).

You studied passages about what to do when you have behaved badly. For this journaling assignment, start with prayer. Ask God to show you to what extent you're living up to the commands we studied in this lesson. Write down anything He shows you that you need to change. Confess your sin to Him and ask Him to forgive you.

 This next step is hard, but worth doing! Make a list of people you have sinned against. Ask God to give you opportunities to ask for their forgiveness and be reconciled to them.

So if you are offering your gift at the altar and there remember that your brother has something against you, leave your gift there before the altar and go. First be reconciled to your brother, and then come and offer your gift (Matthew 5:23-24)

Lesson 12 Wrap Up

 • Write out what you want to remember from Lesson 12.

• What do you want to apply in your life?

• What touched your heart?

• Add to your list of *"What I Learned About God."*

 Write out any verses from Lesson 12 that touched you in a special way.

Did Someone Cause the Death of Your Loved One?

 Do you blame someone for your loved one's death? What are you thinking and feeling about your loss?

Vengeance

 Summarize what you learned about vengeance and how we are to respond when others are at fault.

How are you feeling about all this? If someone caused the death of your loved one, are you willing to trust God to judge them? Are you willing to trust God to do what He knows to be just?

Repay no one evil for evil, but give thought to do what is honorable in the sight of all. If possible, so far as it depends on you, live peaceably with all. Beloved, never avenge yourselves, but leave it to the wrath of God, for it is written, "Vengeance is mine, I will repay, says the Lord" (Romans 12:17-21).

Do you need to forgive someone you believe responsible for your loved one's death? Are you willing to do it now? Ask the Holy Spirit to help you. Write about it or draw a picture.

And whenever you stand praying, forgive, if you have anything against anyone, so that your Father also who is in heaven may forgive you your trespasses (Mark 11:25).

Are you angry with someone? Do you blame someone for the death you are grieving? Write about your feelings and thoughts. Did someone you love take his or her own life? Write about what you learned in this lesson. Then write how you are going to respond to what you learned. Pray and ask God to help you forgive.

Then Peter came up and said to him, "Lord, how often will my brother sin against me, and I forgive him? As many as seven times?" Jesus said to him, "I do not say to you seven times, but seventy times seven" (Mathew 18:21-22).

Lesson 13 Wrap Up

  • Write out what you want to remember from Lesson 13.

• What do you want to apply in your life?

• What touched your heart?

• Add to your list *"What I Learned About God."*

 Write out any verses from Lesson 13 that touched you in a special way.

How Can I Trust God Now?

 Have you trusted God in your grief? Or do you feel like He has let you down? Think about all you have learned thus far in this study. Do you trust God?

Whoever loves father or mother more than me is not worthy of me, and whoever loves son or daughter more than me is not worthy of me. And whoever does not take his cross and follow me is not worthy of me. Whoever finds his life will lose it, and whoever loses his life for my sake will find it (Matthew 10:37-39).

Anger at God

 Summarize what you learned about anger towards God.

And he said to him, "You shall love the Lord your God with all your heart and with all your soul and with all your mind" (Matthew 22:37).

Take time now to write out your thoughts and feelings about what you have read. If you need to, confess your anger to God and that you've been wrong to judge Him. Write out your prayer of confession. Tell Him what you believe about Him.

"Be still, and know that I am God. I will be exalted among the nations, I will be exalted in the earth!" The Lord of hosts is with us; the God of Jacob is our fortress. Selah (Psalm 46:10-11).

Prayer

List what you have learned about prayer. Copy verses that stood out to you. Then write a prayer asking God to help you trust Him. Ask Him to help you pray and to hear His voice.

Do not be anxious about anything, but in everything by prayer and supplication with thanksgiving let your requests be made known to God (Philippians 4:6)

In this lesson, you marked passages from the New Testament and noted their focus. Now read each one aloud. Turn one or more of the ones you love into a prayer for a specific person. Write your prayer.

And when you pray, do not heap up empty phrases as the Gentiles do, for they think that they will be heard for their many words. Do not be like them, for your Father knows what you need before you ask him (Matthew 6:7-8).

A few more of Paul's prayers are 1 Thessalonians 3:12-13, 2 Thessalonians 1:11-12, and Philippians 1:3-6. Using one of these, a favorite Psalm, or one of Paul's greetings, write out a prayer for yourself today. Then write a prayer for someone else.

Grace to you and peace from God our Father and the Lord Jesus Christ, who gave himself for our sins to deliver us from the present evil age, according to the will of our God and Father, to whom be the glory forever and ever (Galatians 1:3-5).

If your church family has been helpful to you in your grief, write about it. Some of us find it hard to write lots of thank-you notes after losing someone we love. Write one thank-you note to your church family expressing how much they mean to you. Perhaps you can list specific things people did to help you. You may want to copy your note and then mail it to your pastor. He will be encouraged by seeing how you were helped.

 If your church did not help you, or if you are not part of a local body of believers, write a prayer asking God to direct you to find a local body-where you can be a part. List friends who you know attend church regularly. Then call one of them to ask if you could go to church with him or her this week.

So if there is any encouragement in Christ, any comfort from love, any participation in the Spirit, any affection and sympathy, complete my joy by being of the same mind, having the same love, being in full accord and of one mind (Philippians 2:1-2).

Lesson 14 Wrap Up

 • Write out what you want to remember about trusting God, prayer, or church from Lesson 14.

• What do you want to apply in your life?

• What touched your heart?

• Add to your list of *"What I Learned About God."*

 Write out any verses from Lesson 14 that touched you in a special way.

Heaven

 Before your loss did you think much about heaven? How has your loss changed what you think or feel about it now?

In my Father's house are many rooms. If it were not so, would I have told you that I go to prepare a place for you? (John 14:2).

Summarize everything you learned about salvation and eternal life. Be sure to reference the verses you studied.

The Lord is not slow to fulfill his promise as some count slowness, but is patient toward you, not wishing that any should perish, but that all should reach repentance (2 Peter 3:9).

Summarize what you learned about the characteristics of children of God. How can you know you are a child of God?

Beloved, let us love one another, for love is from God, and whoever loves has been born of God and knows God (1 John 4:7).

What are you feeling about what you just learned? How are you living up to what you read in Philippians and 2 Corinthians?

 Write about it and ask God to help you apply these truths in your life.

For we know that if the tent that is our earthly home is destroyed, we have a building from God, a house not made with hands, eternal in the heavens (2 Corinthians 5:1).

Heaven

List everything you learned about Heaven.

For to me to live is Christ, and to die is gain (Philippians 1:21).

Write what you are thinking and feeling about heaven. What questions do you still have about it?

But our citizenship is in heaven, and from it we await a Savior, the Lord Jesus Christ, who will transform our lowly body to be like his glorious body, by the power that enables him even to subject all things to himself (Philippians 3:20-21).

Who Goes to Heaven?

 Summarize what you learned about who goes to heaven and who does not.

. . . who desires all people to be saved and to come to the knowledge of the truth. For there is one God, and there is one mediator between God and men, the man Christ Jesus, who gave himself as a ransom for all, which is the testimony given at the proper time (1 Timothy 2:4-6).

And as Moses lifted up the serpent in the wilderness, so must the Son of Man be lifted up, that whoever believes in him may have eternal life (John 3:14-15).

If you are a Christian, take time to write out your testimony regarding when you became a believer. If not, write about that.

Whoever says "I know him" but does not keep his commandments is a liar, and the truth is not in him, but whoever keeps his word, in him truly the love of God is perfected. By this we may know that we are in him: whoever says he abides in him ought to walk in the same way in which he walked (1 John 2:4-6).

Lesson 15 Wrap Up

- Write out what you want to remember from Lesson 15.

- What do you want to apply in your life?

- What touched your heart?

- Add to your list *"What I Learned About God."*

Write out any verses from Lesson 15 that touched you in a special way.

Angels, Mediums, and The Holy Spirit

 What do you know about angels? Think about the Bible stories you've studied over the years. What do you remember about angels from some of these stories?

And to which of the angels has he ever said, "Sit at my right hand until I make your enemies a footstool for your feet"? Are they not all ministering spirits sent out to serve for the sake of those who are to inherit salvation? (Hebrews 1:13-14).

Angels

 Summarize what you learned about angels.

Do you not know that we are to judge angels? How much more, then, matters pertaining to this life! (1 Corinthians 6:3).

Summarize what you learned about the Holy Spirit.

And I will ask the Father, and he will give you another Helper,
to be with you forever (John 14:16).

Seeking Counsel from those in Heaven

 Summarize what you learned about seeking counsel from those in heaven. If you sought the counsel of a sorcerer or medium or if you were or even now are considering it, write what you now know to be true about such things.

Therefore, as you received Christ Jesus the Lord, so walk in him, rooted and built up in him and established in the faith, just as you were taught, abounding in thanksgiving. See to it that no one takes you captive by philosophy and empty deceit, according to human tradition, according to the elemental spirits of the world, and not according to Christ (Colossians 2:6-8).

Lesson 16 Wrap Up

- Write out what you want to remember from Lesson 16.

- What do you want to apply in your life?

- What touched your heart?

- Add to your list *"What I Learned About God."*

- Add to your *"Who I Am In Christ"* list.

Write out any verses from Lesson 16 that touched you in a special way.

How Then Shall We Live?

 Have you been changed by the death of someone you love? List both good and bad ways you see yourself changed. Ask God to show you anything you missed. Be honest in your assessment.

Therefore, my beloved, as you have always obeyed, so now, not only as in my presence but much more in my absence, work out your own salvation with fear and trembling, for it is God who works in you, both to will and to work for his good pleasure (Philippians 2:12-13).

Trials, Temptations, and Suffering

 Summarize what you learned about trials, temptation, and suffering from James 1 and 1 Corinthians 10.

 List some ways you've changed by the death of your loved one.

Therefore let anyone who thinks that he stands take heed lest he fall (1 Corinthians 10:12).

Wisdom

 Summarize what you learned about wisdom.

Let the wise hear and increase in learning, and the one who understands obtain guidance, to understand a proverb and a saying, the words of the wise and their riddles. The fear of the Lord is the beginning of knowledge; fools despise wisdom and instruction (Proverbs 1:5-7).

Bridling The Tongue

 Summarize what you learned about bridling the tongue.

What are you thinking or feeling about what you have learned so far in this lesson? Honestly write out your thoughts.

This is the message we have heard from him and proclaim to you, that God is light, and in him is no darkness at all (1 John 1:5).

You've studied many passages on how to treat others and how we should speak to one another. Do you need to confess anything or talk with God about your speech? Take time to do that now. Write a prayer of confession and ask God to help you change.

But if we walk in the light, as he is in the light, we have fellowship with one another, and the blood of Jesus his Son cleanses us from all sin (1 John 1:7).

Be Doers of the Word: Faith & Works

 Summarize what you learned about *doing* the Word.

Ways I Can Help Others

 You made a list of *"Kind Things Others Did and Said"* earlier (p. 81). Today, make a list of ways you can help others. Then look for ways to do these things.

Be kind to one another, tenderhearted, forgiving one another, as God in Christ forgave you (Ephesians 4:32).

Wait Patiently and Do What Is Right

 Summarize what you learned about waiting patiently and doing what is right.

Are you waiting patiently for the coming of the Lord? Write what is going on with you today. How are you handling your grief today? Are you seeing the good that God is doing in you as you seek Him, study His Word and apply truth in your life?

For in this hope we were saved. Now hope that is seen is not hope. For who hopes for what he sees? But if we hope for what we do not see, we wait for it with patience (Romans 8:24-25).

Lesson 17 Wrap Up

- Write out what you want to remember from Lesson 17.

- What do you want to apply in your life?

- What touched your heart?

- Add to your list of *"What I Learned About God."*

Write out any verses from Lesson 17 that touched you in a special way.

Bless the Lord, O My Soul

 Have you been able to praise God while grieving? How has your loss affected your prayer life and the way you worship Him? As you look back through this study, can you list things God has done for you? Are you able to see His work in your life when grieving?

Bless the LORD, O my soul, and all that is within me, bless his holy name! Bless the LORD, O my soul, and forget not all his benefits (Psalm 103:2).

Psalm 103

 Summarize what you learned from your study of Psalm 103.

Are you able to praise God for His benefits today? Write a poem or prayer expressing your praise.

Bless the Lord, all his works, in all places of his dominion. Bless the Lord, O my soul!
(Psalm 103:22).

Psalm 23

 Summarize what you learned about Psalm 23.

Look back in your *Journal* at what you wrote about what healing might look like. This was one of the exercises early in this study. Having studied God's Word, do you see God healing you in your grief? If so, write about how He has healed you. Or write out a prayer asking Him to heal you and to show you what you need to do to aid in your healing.

Not only that, but we rejoice in our sufferings, knowing that suffering produces endurance, and endurance produces character, and character produces hope, and hope does not put us to shame, because God's love has been poured into our hearts through the Holy Spirit who has been given to us (Romans 5:3-5).

Sheep and the Good Shepherd

 Summarize what you learned about the sheep and the Good Shepherd.

How can you apply what you learned from John 10 in your life?

My sheep hear my voice, and I know them, and they follow me. I give them eternal life, and they will never perish, and no one will snatch them out of my hand (John 10:27-28).

From *God's Healing in Grief—*

Dear one, if your loved ones were believers in Jesus Christ, if they were Christians, Jesus knows them and He gave them eternal life. No one is able to snatch them out of the Father's hand. They are okay; you have no need to worry or be concerned about them. They are in the presence of Christ and will live eternally with God. But while you are living in your earthy body, you still have work to do.

As a child of God and believer in Christ, God's love for you is higher than the heavens. He has removed your transgressions from you as far as the east is from the west. God has redeemed you from the pit and crowns you with love and mercy. You are His sheep. All who are His sheep hear His voice and follow Him. As you follow Him and obey His commands you will be transformed into His image. He is a good shepherd who will restore your soul even in the midst of grief and suffering. Will you resist God's work in your life? Will you apply what you have learned in this study in your life as you heal and find hope, peace, and joy?

> [21] For to this you have been called, because Christ also suffered for you,
>
> leaving you an example, so that you might follow in his steps.
>
> [22] He committed no sin, neither was deceit found in his mouth.
>
> [23] When he was reviled, he did not revile in return;
>
> when he suffered, he did not threaten,
>
> but continued entrusting himself to him who judges justly.
>
> [24] He himself bore our sins in his body on the tree,
>
> that we might die to sin and live to righteousness.
>
> By his wounds you have been healed.
>
> [25] For you were straying like sheep,
>
> but have now returned to the Shepherd and Overseer of your souls.
>
> (1 Peter 2:21-25)

We are called to follow Christ and become like Him. As you grow to be like Christ through grief and suffering, will you follow His example, beloved? He bore our sins that we might die to sin and live to righteousness. He came to give us eternal life, a wonderful life that begins at the moment of salvation. You do not have to wait until you reach heaven to begin to walk in the Spirit and live by the Spirit. You can begin today.

We pray you will.

Write out a prayer of thanksgiving for all the Lord taught you in this study and for what He has done for you.

Lesson 18 Wrap Up

- Write out what you want to remember from Lesson 18.

- What do you want to apply in your life?

- What touched your heart?

- Add to your list *"What I Learned About God."*

Write out any verses from Lesson 18 that touched you in a special way.

Wrap Up

Time to look back at the lists you made. Think about all you have learned from studying God's Word. Then look at what you wrote in this Journal about what healing will look like for you. How are you doing? Have you begun to see God's healing in your life? Are you confident in what you have learned through this study?

Look through each lesson in this study. Write one truth you want to remember from each lesson.

Lesson 1

Lesson 2

Lesson 3

Lesson 4

Lesson 5

Lesson 6

Lesson 7

Lesson 8

Lesson 9

Lesson 10

Lesson 11

Lesson 12

Lesson 13

Lesson 14

Lesson 15

Lesson 16

Lesson 17

Lesson 18

What are some things you want to take away from this study? How has it helped you in your grief? Where are you today compared to where you were when you started this study?

Have you seen God's healing in your grief?

 Thank Him for all He is doing in and through you.